I0486174

Conversation Skills Now!

Ignite Your Life With Proven Conversation Strategies, Communication Skills, And Conversation Power To Create Your Destiny!

Mia Conrad

STOP!!! Before you read any further....Would you like to know the Secrets of Transforming your life, overcome insecurities, develop leadership skills, and undeniable confidence in your personal, professional, and relationship life?

If your answer is yes, then you are not alone. Thousands of people are looking for the secret to have unstoppable confidence and self-driven power in all areas of their lives.

If you have been searching for these answers without much luck, you're in the right place!

Not only will you gain incredible insight in this book, but because I want to make sure to give you as much value as possible, right now for a limited time you can get full **100% FREE access to a VIP bonus EBook** entitled **LIMITLESS ENERGY!**

Legal Notice

Disclaimer Notice

Table Of Contents

Introduction

I want to thank you and congratulate you for purchasing the book, "Conversation Skills Now! - Ignite Your Life With Proven Conversation Strategies, Communication Skills, And Conversation Power To Create Your Destiny".

This book contains insight on the Art of Conversation and how you can use this art to create a life of your choosing.

Picture this; you are standing in an elevator with a middle aged man wearing a Hawaiian shirt, shorts, and boat shoes. You say nothing to him, you do however, think to yourself, "Wow, pretty relaxed attire for a Tuesday afternoon, he must be out of work."

Now consider this, chances are this middle aged man in relaxed attire is not out of work, on the contrary. You see, he is actually the owner of one of the area's finest business enterprises. He is actually so successful that he doesn't have to dress up, but you wouldn't know this, because you didn't bother to talk to him. If you would have spoken to him, you would have found out that he actually was in need of someone like you.

Whether you are young, old, successful, unsuccessful, an entrepreneur, or an employee, you owe it to yourself and your future to learn and apply the art of conversation to your advantage. This book shows you how.

Thanks again for purchasing this book. I hope you enjoy it!

Chapter 1: The Importance Of Conversation

It is said that humans are extremely conversational animals. Other than the ability to think, one of the things that make humans stand out from other animals is their ability to make conversations with others. This ability has proven to be the backbone of society, as interactions between different individuals is very important in forming all kinds of social bonds.

Of course, it is not that conversation is merely a domain reserved for humans. In fact, even other animals have shown their own unique ability to converse. While they don't do it the same way humans do, animals have their own unique way of communicating with each other. These communication skills allow them to form groups for defense, attack, and other kinds of tasks and tactics. Communication has allowed these organisms to have an extra edge in the wild, where numbers and coordination can spell the difference between life and death.

When you look back at human history, it is apparent that humans have utilized the power of communication to the hilt as well. While the earliest humans have languages that are far from the language systems used today, the presence of these communication systems, both written and oral, cannot be denied.

Perhaps more importantly, not only did conversation allowed for talking, but it also allowed for the sharing of history, virtually assuring that the existence of our forefathers will never be forgotten. Oral histories abound in all ethnic groups worldwide, and a lot of them are more or less proven by the presence of relics in different cradles of civilizations. Re-tracing history, and perhaps the interest in tracing it, probably would have not existed without the presence of our innate communication skills.

But while there are many sub-uses of communication, its main value still lies on its ability to bring people closer together thru communication. As you would know by now, the best way to get to know a person is to talk to them. Of course, you can always choose to not talk to them, but you may actually miss out on a life-changing experience.

If there is an everyday skill that you must continually practice, it is your communication skills. Applying the art of conversation to your everyday life can help you create your destiny in ways you never thought possible. In the next chapters, you will learn the different skills you'll need to talk to anyone. You'll also learn how you can cultivate different personality traits that make you an effective conversationalist. And last but not least, this article will teach you how to use your conversational skill as a means to highlight yourself.

Chapter 2: The Characteristics Of A Great Conversationalist

Everyone has the ability to start and make a conversation, but only a few can actually be said to be skilled at it. Furthermore, only a handful of people are said to be exceptional when it comes to making conversations. Some would say that the members of this handful are born with exceptional skills of conversation. Others would say that just like any technique, conversational skills can be worked on.

Regardless of which side of the fence you are on, there are distinct characteristics any great conversationalist possesses. And if you can have one, some, or even all of these characteristics, chances are you will be very successful in conversing.

The following is a list of characteristics of a great conversationalist.

1. Speech skills

This is the most obvious trait any good conversationalist has. While everybody has the ability to speak, not everybody has the ability to express themselves thru words. Also, not everybody has the ability to get their message across in the most effective way. A great conversationalist has a way with speaking. They know how to express thoughts using both verbal and non-verbal cues, getting their message across to a wide variety of individuals.

2. Listening skills

A conversation is more than just talking. One must also be a skilled listener in order to be a good conversationalist. The best conversationalists are great in reading the thoughts of the people they are talking to, whether they are expressing it through their words or non-verbal actions such as their reactions and body language. One part of creating optimal conversational flow is to understand the balance between expressing your thoughts and listening to what the other person/s have to say.

3. Mastery of language

It is simply logical for the best conversationalists to have a command of language. For a person to make the transition to becoming a great conversationalist in a particular language, he/she must attain a certain level of mastery in using it. Of course, that would involve having a deep knowledge of the different words, but perhaps more importantly one must know exactly when to use these words. Mastery of words is not reflected on having the most elaborate vocabulary; it's more about using the right words at the right time.

4. Experience

To attain perfection in any kind of skill, one must consistently practice it. Practicing your communication skills will help in development. You can do self-study and training on this one, but nothing beats actually being exposed in situations where you'll have to talk your way into the crowd, so to speak. There are many ways experience can help you become a great conversationalist. You're able to meet different people, learn different effective approaches, and correct mistakes and weaknesses.

5. Confidence

Being confident is something that can be extremely helpful for all levels of conversation. Because of either being pressured or being too self-conscious, some people have shaky confidence when they are talking. Lack of confidence can impact one's speaking impact. It can cause the speaker to say what they don't mean and it can also cause the listener to interpret the message the wrong way. For the message to be sent correctly and emphatically, you must deliver your message with confidence and conviction.

6. A feel for the crowd

May it be talking to a single person or to a crowd, a good conversationalist has a good feel for the crowd. Before they even start talking, a conversationalist observes the person/group he/she is talking to, with the aim of determining the best conversational approach possible. Having a feel for the crowd is not only about wordplay. Actually, it's predicated more in people knowledge. If you know

how to relate with the people you're talking to, chances are your conversation will be a complete success.

Chapter 3: The Elements Of Conversation

Conversation is consisted of different elements. Each of these elements plays a huge role in sending your message across. If there is one thing about actual, face-to-face conversation, more elements are in play, and therefore the conversation actually becomes more dynamic. There are different elements to take account for during a conversation. Each of these elements can either make or break the effectiveness of your dialogue. For reference, here are 4 of the most important elements of effective conversation.

1. Tone

As most experts would say, it is not just about what you say, but it is also about how you say it. Your tone has a huge impact on how your message will be received by the masses. Your tone can have a profound effect on how people may perceive what you are saying, regardless if it is spoken in English or any other type of language. Because of this, one must know by heart how particular words are spoken as to prevent misinterpretations. In addition, adjusting the volume, speed, and intonation of speaking can give emphasis on what you exactly mean when you speak.

2. Eye contact

This is something very unique with personal conversations, and this can make or break the effectiveness of your talk. The way your eyes make contact to your audience (especially if it is a one-on-one conversation) has a huge impact on how convincing your message will ultimately be. How the speaker and listener's eye makes contact with each other is a huge barometer of interest for both sides of the conversation. According to a study, regular eye contact encourages participation, so make sure you give your listeners a steady dose of eye contact when you talk.

3. Body Language

Conversation experts will point to 2 cues regarding conversations: verbal and non-verbal cues. While you speak with verbal actions, your non-verbal actions also tell the story. If you are confident and you know what you are talking about, your body language will show it. If you are unfocused, unsure, or rattled, it will show in your body as well. Actions such as fidgeting, slouching, and erratic eye movement can speak different messages ranging from unpreparedness to disrespect. In contrast, the proper use of hand and body movement while you speak makes your speech sound more honest and convincing.

4. Spontaneity

A good conversation is both spontaneous and free-flowing. In contrast, having one lull too many combined with the use of some "canned" answers can greatly detract from the conversation experience. Because of this, one must develop their spontaneity to keep things interesting and lively. There are 3 ways to have superior spontaneity while talking: deep knowledge and understanding, supreme confidence, and not being too self-conscious. All these traits can be developed, and can bring great results when executed the right way.

Chapter 4: Working On Your Conversational Skills

Being an expert conversationalist doesn't happen overnight. Even those who have a gift with starting a conversation had to constantly work on their skills to reach such a level that they can express themselves well in public. Fortunately, improving on your conversational skills is not as tedious as it may initially seem. But of course, it will take a conscious effort in your part to continuously improve on your conversational skills.

Not a lot of people know how to improve on their conversational skills and at the same time highlight what they have to offer to others. Just like in most affairs, it takes a conscious effort to actually become a more capable conversationalist. Here are some of the tips you can use to become better at conversations and expressing yourself.

1. Actively converse everyday

Just like muscles, your conversational skills can get built with practice and can be broken down by misuse. Because of this, the best way you can improve your conversational skills well is by continually engaging yourself to conversations. May it be to your family members and friends to colleagues and business partners, initiating and participating in conversations provides ways to improve both your speaking and listening skills. And as a bonus, you get to learn more about different things in life.

2. Realize your strengths and weaknesses as a conversationalist

It is so tough to perfect one's conversational skills, and even then there's no such thing as a perfect conversation. Every person has their own unique set of strengths and weaknesses as a conversationalist. And continually working on and around both can help you constantly improve your conversational skills. You must make a constant effort to highlight and further strengthen your strengths, and at the same time improve your weaknesses.

3. Improve your self-confidence

Being comfortable with yourself is very important if you are aiming to become a great conversationalist. There will be times where you'll be confronting strangers, if not huge crowds. And there would always be self-doubt if you'll be able to assert yourself when approaching your target audience. Overall self-confidence can help you immensely when approaching others. Feeling good about yourself will allow you to have a more natural flow of talking. Also, it will make you less tentative as you'll think less about what others think or say about you.

4. Improve your way with words

Language can be quite a tricky thing to learn. As this is a form of applied knowledge, it takes time to actually understand how to use it perfectly. The best way to improve your way of words is to continuously find ways to work on it. Familiarizing yourself with words by means of reading, exposing yourself to media in that language, and simply getting used to the language's unique nuances will greatly help you in perfecting both your speaking and comprehension skills.

5. Know your audience

Understanding who you are talking to is a very important element of the conversation process. If you don't know who you are talking to, chances are you won't get your message across effectively. This is where one's people knowledge comes into the picture. Beyond just speaking your piece, you must also understand the particular needs of the person you're talking to. You must cater your conversational strategy according to who you are talking to. It's the best way to get across them and have a successful conversation.

6. Never let conversation become a one-way street

A conversation where only one side is operating is not effective. If you or the other person is the one who's talking all the time, then something is going wrong with your conversation. To encourage a healthy conversation, one of the best ways to do it is by keeping things lively. You must talk in such a way that they'll be encouraged to participate actively. At the same time, when they are talking, make sure to listen and insert your own thoughts when the opportunity shows

 itself. As a speaker/listener, you have the power to make any conversation interesting for both parties.

7. Present yourself well

When starting or joining a conversation, you must present yourself well. Proper presentation will send a message to others that you mean business, so to speak. The best way to present yourself is to dress up according to the occasion, make a smooth entry, make sure to create proper eye contact with the one/s you'll be talking to, and introduce yourself. Also, make sure to introduce yourself well, being self-assured without being self-absorbed. Proper self-presentation is the first step towards starting a conversation and perhaps acquiring lasting acquaintances.

8. Never stop learning

This is where accumulated knowledge and wisdom can come into the picture. What you know and what you have learned will show on how you talk. Because of this, you should never stop learning while you're at it. You can learn different things from the people you know and the things you observe. The best way to continuously learn is to keep an open mind. Even though you may have amassed all kinds of knowledge and accomplished all kinds of things, you must always be open to the notion that you can still learn more.

Chapter 5: How To Speak With Strangers Successfully

"Don't talk to strangers". That is what the old adage says. While there are times when this quote holds absolute truth, there would be times when you absolutely need to talk to a stranger. And for some people who are not used to doing it, this could be especially difficult. This chapter will be your step-by-step process on how to speak with strangers successfully.

Why is learning how to speak with strangers a complete necessity? It is mainly because there are a lot of situations in life that absolutely calls for it. Take for example going into a gala, a family reunion, or a job interview. There is a very good chance you'll know absolutely no one in these occasions. If you do not know how to speak with strangers (or at least not comfortable enough to speak with strangers), chances are you'll remain alone or you won't be able to accomplish whatever you set out to do. To prevent such an awkward situation from happening, one must work on their ability to converse with strangers.

Other than the occasional meeting with strangers, there is another solid importance with having the knowledge of striking a conversation with a stranger. In the work setting, in social gatherings, and even while walking on the street, you'll never know who you are going to meet. You'll never know if that person sitting next to you on the table, on the elevator, or on the lines is someone that can change your life. And you just might miss out on that opportunity because you don't know how to speak with them.

Never miss out an opportunity to know someone and express yourself by learning how to speak well with strangers. This step-by-step process will help you talk to strangers in no time.

1. Know the setting

The setting will dictate what kind of approach you should be taking and how you can present yourself to the occasion. If it is a corporate meeting or interview, you may want to make yourself presentable by wearing appropriate attire and by talking in a more formal manner. If it is a party or a gathering, a more relaxed approach is better. After all, everyone attending such events is there to unwind and have a good time. And if you are in a public place such as a street or a mall, it's best to establish yourself first in a friendly manner before you even start talking.

2. Know how to begin

People say that first impressions last. This is especially true when it comes to talking to strangers, as they tend to remember you on how you approach them the very first time. Because of this, you have to know how to approach a person well. The best way to do that is by establishing eye contact with them before you even mention a word. This will grab their attention and will set the mood straight that you want to talk to them. Once you get your attention, start the conversation in a lively and confident way. Saying hello and introducing yourself will suffice on most occasions.

3. Begin with small talk

While most people don't like the concept of small talk, this is actually a solid technique when trying to know someone or at least start a conversation. Small talk allows you to get to know the person little by little, and can open up opportunities to talk about bigger things as you progress with the conversation. One of the best ways to begin small talk is to ask them how they are doing, what they are doing in life, and the things they are interested in. Listen well to their answers as you can use them later on in your conversation. At the same time, expect that they'll ask you the same things.

4. Gamely answer questions

When they are asking you questions, it probably means that they are interested in your company. When they ask you questions, the best thing you can do is to answer them in the best way you can. Never allow for a dull moment during conversation as it can give off an aura that either you are not interested or you are lying to them. You can even answer in a witty way if the situation calls for it as it can lighten the mood for both speaker and listener.

5. Beware of the non-verbal cues

Be conscious about how you express yourself thru non-verbal cues. You may sound interesting and enthusiastic when you speak. But if your body language says otherwise, you'll still come off as someone who is generally disinterested. Avoid body language that may indicate that you're indifferent such as rolling eyes, yawning, and being distracted by outside factors such as mobile devices. Maintain eye contact and good posture at all times. Smile a genuine smile and make them comfortable when they are speaking.

6. Share something about yourself

Even when they are not asking, it will be nice if you'll tell them something about yourself. You can share some very basic information and you can tell some random stories about yourself. Make sure to tell it in a tone that you won't come out as someone who is arrogant or self-absorbed. Remember that the main reason why you're doing this step is mainly to help others to get to know you, not to turn them off right at the gates.

7. Be sincere and honest

In a world full of strangers, turncoats, and self-promoters, sincerity and honesty is quickly becoming such a rare trait. You'll need to show throughout your conversation that you are sincere and honest with what you are saying. It is the easiest way for you to start a conversation and possibly start something more meaningful beyond that. Throughout the conversation, remember the quote *"Mean what you say and say what you mean"*.

8. End the conversation on a high note

Of course, there would come a time that the conversation shall end. And in order to be remembered, you must make sure to end the conversation on a high note. The best way to end the conversation is to politely say goodbye. Make sure to show them that you appreciated the conversation you had. And last but not least, open up to the chance of going further acquainted with ways such as exchanging phone numbers.

Conclusion

Thank you again for purchasing this book!

I hope this book was able to help you understand how the Art of Conversation can be of extreme use in your life and help you create the life of your dreams.

Striking up a conversation with a stranger might be the hardest thing you have to do in everyday life, but it still is a very important part of identifying opportunities.

It is true that you will not become an excellent conversationalist in one day, but with and enhanced self belief and regular conversations, over time you will improve! So use what you have learned in this book and start to initiate a conversation the right way.

Also, if you know of anyone else that might enjoy reading this book, please inform them of it so they can be on their way to better conversations and success.

Finally, if you enjoyed this book, please take the time to share your thoughts and post a review on Amazon. It'd be greatly appreciated!

Thank you and good luck!

Preview Of:

<u>Happiness Now</u>

Secrets From The Happiest People On Earth

Introduction

I want to thank you and congratulate you for purchasing the book **Happiness:** *Secrets From The Happiest People On Earth*. This book contains information about the Happiest People on Earth, as well as, insights on how you can apply these same principles to your life!

If you want to be happy, you have to first ask yourself what it is that's making you feel blue. Before you trek the path that will help you solve your issues, you have to be totally rid of conflict with who you are. If the kind of happy you want to experience is unadulterated, being honest with yourself is the starting point.

Are you down because you're discontented with your position in life? Has your partner left you? Have you moved to another city and haven't coped with the changes yet? Do you think that the number of friends you have isn't enough? Or are you still grieving the death of a family member?

For whatever reason it is, you have to admit that being sad bites. Seeing the world in a gloomy perspective is tough. Rather than continue with your ways, consider giving yourself a break. Way too many times, it has been said that life is short. So why waste moments being stuck in a downward spiral?

Here are 15 of the happiest people on earth. From social workers, artists, and businessmen to athletes and musicians, you can get some much-needed tips. Taking a peek at their situations in life may just open your eyes to what you deem to be the problem in yours.

Thanks again for purchasing this book. I hope you enjoy it!

Chapter 1 – The Joy In Social Work

"True happiness comes from the joy of deeds well done, the zest of creating things new." -Antoine de Saint-Exupery

Social workers are among the happiest on earth because they know that by doing another a favor, they are doing themselves a much bigger favor. They aren't oblivious to the fact that the rewards of making people's day are incomparable. These people are happy because they have made way for others to smile. Like them, if you're desperate for some mood-lifting, try clearing your schedule, be spontaneous, and cheer someone up. In your own way, you should take steps to change the world too.

Happy Person #1: Desmond Tutu

As a South African social rights activist, Desmond Tutu rose to fame. He helped his fellowmen by fighting against AIDS, poverty, racism, and sexism. He also opposed the Apartheid revolution and won the 1984 Nobel Peace Prize for it. While living with his wife and Children in Cape Town, his days aren't spent sad because he is confident that he served as oppressed people's voice.

Happy Person #2: Eva Peron

Eva Peron, the 2nd wife of the Argentine president Juan Peron, was a jolly fellow as she made a difference in the lives of the working class Argentines. She ran charities, supervised government agencies in labor and health, and initiated the Female Peronist Party, the first large-scale group that championed women's suffrage.

Happy Person #3: Mother Teresa

After having founded organizations that arranged hospices for people with HIV, leprosy, and tuberculosis, Mother Teresa discovered happiness in serving others. For her, selflessness nurtures good karma and seeing the positive effects of her actions is priceless. As she dedicated her life to charity work, she proclaimed that she belongs to the world.

Why Would Kindness Make You Happy?

Kindness will make you happy as it lets you discover inner peace. It allows you to sort things out while showing you a picture of yourself as a good person. Especially if you're the type who is usually apathetic, kindness will benefit you. It gives you the idea that you are bigger than you imagined yourself to be. Also, you have to admit that if you were the one in need, you'll be made happy if someone did the same to you.

Ten Acts of Kindness You Can Do

1. Buy lunch for a homeless person.

2. Do a week's worth of laundry for a family member.

3. Donate blood.

4. Gather old clothes and give it to the less fortunate.

5. Give a waiter a generous tip.

6. Listen intently to someone's problems.

7. Leave extra money on a vending machine.

8. Pay the toll fee for the vehicle-owner behind you.

9. Run errands for a neighbor.

10. Visit an orphanage and bring with you some goodies.

Thanks for Previewing My Exciting book Entitled:

"Happiness Now!"

To purchase this book, simply go to the Amazon Kindle store and simply search:

"HAPPINESS NOW!"

Then just scroll down until you see my book. You will know it is mine because you will see my name "Mia Conrad" underneath the title.

Alternatively, you can visit my author page on Amazon to see this book and other work I have done. Thanks so much, and please don't forget your free bonuses

DON'T LEAVE YET! - CHECK OUT YOUR FREE BONUSES BELOW!

Free Bonus Offer: Get Free Access To The PotentialRise.com VIP Newsletter!

Once you enter your email address you will immediately get free access to this awesome newsletter!

But wait, right now if you join now for free you will also get free access to the "LIMITLESS ENERGY" free EBook!

To claim both your FREE VIP NEWSLETTER MEMBERSHIP and your FREE BONUS Ebook on LIMITLESS ENERGY!

Just Go To:

www.PotentialRise.com

www.ingramcontent.com/pod-product-compliance
Lightning Source LLC
Chambersburg PA
CBHW070758180526
45168CB00004B/1662